IN WINTER, Where Do They Go?

Thirteen-Lined Ground Squirrels

by J. Clark Sawyer

Consultant: Scott R. Craven
Professor Emeritus
Department of Forest and Wildlife Ecology
University of Wisconsin
Madison, Wisconsin

BEARPORT PUBLISHING

New York, New York

Credits

TOC, © All Canada Photos/Glow; 4–5, © Jim McKinley/Getty Images; 6, © encikAn/Shutterstock; 6–7, © Miller, Brian K./Animals Animals/Earth Scenes; 8–9, © Wayne Lynch/All Canada Photos/ Corbis; 9, © John T. Williams; 11, © Photo by H. Carey, University of Wisconsin–Madison; 12, © John M. Burnley/Science Photo Library; 13, © Photo by H. Carey, University of Wisconsin– Madison; 14–15, © Kolar, Richard/Animals Animals/Earth Scenes; 16–17, © Tripp Davenport Uvalde Texas; 18–19, © Ian Maton/Shutterstock; 20, © Lisa Tretiak/Prairie Wildlife Rehabilitation Centre; 21, © Jim McKinley/Getty Images; 22T, © Shattil & Rozinski/naturepl.com; 22B, © Chamelion Studio/Shutterstock; 23TL, © iStockphoto/Thinkstock; 23TR, © iStockphoto/ Thinkstock; 23BL, © Photo by H. Carey, University of Wisconsin–Madison; 23BR, © iStockphoto/ Thinkstock.

Publisher: Kenn Goin
Editor: Jessica Rudolph
Creative Director: Spencer Brinker
Design: Debrah Kaiser
Photo Researcher: Michael Win

Library of Congress Cataloging-in-Publication Data

Clark Sawyer, J., author.
  Thirteen-lined ground squirrels / by J. Clark Sawyer.
      pages cm. — (In winter, where do they go?)
  Includes bibliographical references and index.
  ISBN-13: 978-1-62724-317-9 (library binding)
  ISBN-10: 1-62724-317-8 (library binding)
  1. Thirteen-lined ground squirrel—Juvenile literature. 2. Ground squirrels—Juvenile literature.
I. Title.
  QL737.R68C54 2015
  599.36'5—dc23
                                    2014009027

For more information, write to Bearport Publishing Company, Inc., 45 West 21st Street, Suite 3B, New York, New York 10010. Printed in the United States of America.

10 9 8 7 6 5 4 3 2 1

Contents

Thirteen-Lined Ground Squirrels

It's a fall day in a grassy field.

A thirteen-lined ground squirrel looks for food.

It's getting ready for winter.

Thirteen-lined ground squirrels have 13 light and dark stripes. This is how they got their name.

The small squirrel eats a lot.

It feeds on seeds and **insects**, such as crickets.

Eating a lot of food helps it build up body fat.

cricket

Ground squirrels have pouches in their cheeks. They carry food in them.

Ground squirrels live in underground homes called **burrows**.

They sleep and stay safe there.

Just before winter, a squirrel brings grass into its home.

It makes a soft bed.

Ground squirrel burrows have many openings, tunnels, and rooms.

a ground squirrel poking
its head out of a burrow

The squirrel curls up into a little ball.

It rests on its bed of grass.

The squirrel is **hibernating**.

Before hibernating, ground squirrels block burrow openings with dirt. This keeps other animals out.

The squirrel stays in its burrow all winter. Why?

There is very little food in cold winter months.

The squirrel hibernates until spring.

There will be more food then.

Other animals also hibernate. For example, some kinds of bats hibernate in caves.

All winter, the squirrel eats nothing!

How does it stay alive?

It lives off fat from its body.

The food that squirrels eat in warm months builds up fat. Their bodies use fat as food during hibernation.

In spring, the little squirrel wakes up.

It digs through the dirt at one of the burrow openings.

Then it pokes its head out.

Ground squirrels can hibernate for up to six months. In warm months, they sleep in their burrows only at night.

The squirrel has not eaten for many months.

It doesn't weigh much.

It is very hungry.

During hibernation, ground squirrels may lose half their body weight.

Outside, flowers **bloom**.

Crickets hop around.

The squirrel runs off to find a meal!

In the spring, female squirrels raise babies in their burrows.

ground squirrel babies

Thirteen-Lined Ground Squirrel Facts

There are more than 60 kinds of ground squirrels. They live all over the world. Thirteen-lined ground squirrels live in the grassy areas of central North America.

Where thirteen-lined ground squirrels live

Food: Grasses, flowers, seeds, fruits, vegetables, worms, caterpillars, crickets, beetles, mice, bird eggs, and baby birds

Length: About 10 inches (25.4 cm), including the tail

Weight: About 8 ounces (227 g)

Life Span: Around six to seven years

Cool Fact: The stripes and dots on the fur of thirteen-lined ground squirrels help them to blend into grasses. This makes it very difficult for hawks, coyotes, snakes, and other enemies to see them.

Size of an adult thirteen-lined ground squirrel

A teacup

Glossary

bloom (BLOOM) to open into flowers

burrows (BUR-ohz) holes or tunnels dug by animals to live in

hibernating (HYE-bur-*nayt*-ing) spending the winter in a cold, inactive state

insects (IN-sekts) small animals that have six legs, three main body parts, two antennae, and a hard covering called an exoskeleton

Index

Read More

Boring, Mel. *Rabbits, Squirrels, and Chipmunks (Young Naturalist Field Guides).* Milwaukee, WI: Gareth Stevens (2000).

Swanson, Diane. *Squirrels.* Milwaukee, WI: Gareth Stevens (2003).

Learn More Online

To learn more about thirteen-lined ground squirrels, visit
www.bearportpublishing.com/InWinterWhereDoTheyGo?

About the Author

J. Clark Sawyer lives in Connecticut. She has edited and written many books about history, science, and nature for children.